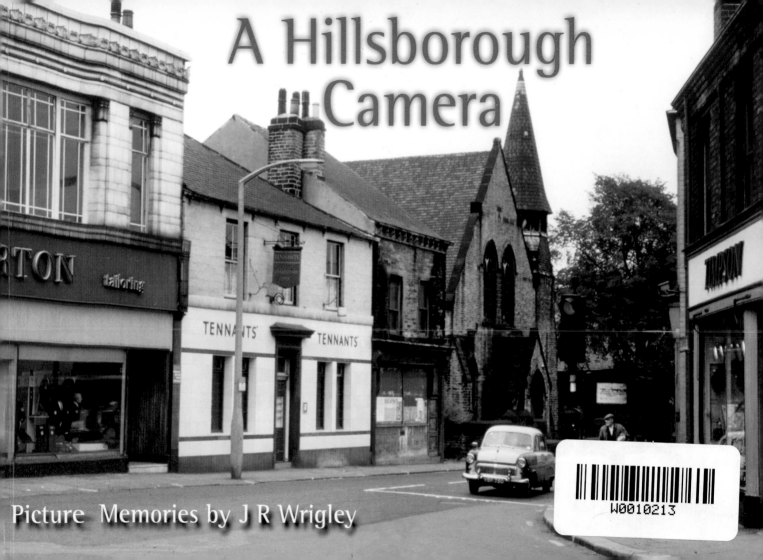

# A Hillsborough Camera

Picture Memories by J R Wrigley

ISBN 0 9534267 3 X

Printed in 2003 by Pickard Publishing

Published & Printed by Pickard Publishing,
10-11 Riverside Park, Sheaf Gardens, Sheffield S2 4BB
Telephone 0114 275 7222 or 275 7444
Facsimile 0114 275 8866

9780095 44455

# Introduction

Unlike my previous book, "An Ecclesfield Camera" I cannot claim to have taken all the photographs in the book. Some of them are before my time but I thought them worth including.

There is no defining where Hillsborough begins and ends. Unlike postal districts it has no boundaries. The name originated when the owner of a newly built hall on what were than the outskirts of Sheffield decided to name it after Hillsborough Castle in County Down, Ireland. The hall is now Hillsborough Library in Hillsborough Park.

Hillsborough Corner is a good starting place for a book about Hillsborough and I have taken as the area Langsett Road, Holme Lane to Malin Bridge, Middlewood Road as far as the old Hillsborough Park Cinema, Bradfield Road and Penistone Road between Leppings Lane and Hillfoot Bridge.

Hillsborough has also now become familiar to football fans as a well-known ground though when I was young it was always referred to as Owlerton. (Hence "The Owls"). I have here a number of photographs that I think will be of interest whether you are a supporter of the club or not.

I have tried to arrange the photographs in some sort of logical order - mostly by area.

I was born in the area and my family's roots are here. It has not changed as much as some parts of the city but I hope what follows will stir a few memories.

*Front Cover.*
Bradfield Road from Hillsborough corner as it was in 1968. "Let Burton's dress you" was an advertising slogan prior to World War Two. The Methodist church stood where the Wilko store now stands.

Hillsborough Bridge is viewed from Walkley Lane some time before the First World War. Blanchard Bros. have a prominent notice for their shop on Infirmary Road.

No. 425 Langsett Road - The Wrigley Family 1905

Mrs Wrigley standing outside the house around 1936.

Back row (l to r) William (died 1907), John (my father - wounded on Hill 60 1915), Joseph (killed on the first day of the Somme July 1st 1916), Ernest (was wounded in France 1916)
Front row: Robert (enlisted at 15 years of age but survived) John Wrigley (father - served with Gordon Relief Expedition, 1885)
Nellie (became Lady Almoner at the Jessop Hospital), Hannah (Mother) Richard (wounded at Gallipoli, later gassed in France)

Almost opposite No. 425 was the entrance to Hillsborough Barracks. Through this gate would come the regimental band followed by soldiers in their dress uniforms on their way to church parade at Owlerton Church, watched by a crowd of onlookers.

This tram is heading for Hillsborough Corner and has just passed the Barracks. This picture was taken some time in the '30s.

A photograph of Barrack Hill looking downhill. On the left (marked with a cross) stands Elsie Wells (born Ovendale). This information is given on the back of the card with the date written as 1910.

No. 364 Langsett Road at the corner of Bamforth Street where Arthur Holliday had his "Collectors' Corner". It was a fascinating shop - in the days before "The Antiques Road Show" when real treasures were well within the means of the ordinary collector. Arthur priced them in guineas rather than pounds. Half-a-guinea (52p) was a common price. Here was Satsuma, Nanking porcelain, old wood carvings, tapestries and samplers, seaside souvenirs, paintings and watercolours - a host of collectibles at reasonable prices.

He mostly had a cigar in his hands which he

waved to emphasise a point or, in the saleroom, to indicate a bid. An invitation into his back room was a compliment and here he would keep any especial treasure to show to "the trade".

His political opinions were to the right and he could be coaxed to express them with some vehemence.

He was an honest man and a fair man. He lived and died in Bradfield Road flats. After his death his wife kept the shop open for a time but the business was Arthur and it was not long before the gate went up for the last time. It stood derelict for a few years but was eventually demolished to make way for the new slip road for traffic going down to Penistone Road. The next time you drive that way spare a thought for another bit of lost Sheffield.

This shows Langsett Road at Woodland Street. On the right is the old tollhouse and next to it is the Victoria Vaults public house. On the other side of Woodland Street was a beer-off shop and beyond that is the Wycliffe Congregational chapel. Everything on this photograph has gone with the exception of the tollhouse.

No. 358 Langsett Road. These small drink shops were common up to the 1970s. Jack's shop was typical. Here young bloods could down a pint of Sarsaparilla when they would have been shown the door in a pub. Vimto was another beverage and could be had hot on a cold day. The purchase of condoms by the more daring was probably made more in hope than expectation.

Patnick's shop occupied three or four houses in addition to the shop front. It was a veritable warren inside and once in it wasn't easy to find your way back to the entrance. But for the book and record collector it was a kind of collector's heaven. One memory is of Aaron Patnick tearing up old cartons in a back room and feeding them onto an already-blazing fire until you feared that the whole place would go up.
It never did!

Standing at Channing Street and looking towards Bamforth Street there are some familiar shops that have now disappeared from our streets - Gallons and Parkins and Davy's and others supplying the needs of the many terraced houses that crowded behind Langsett Road. Demolition and the rise of the motor car and supermarket spelt death for many of these shops and the character of those that remain has changed completely.

Nos. 320-322 was Lingard's, the ironmongers. This fine old firm is in the 1905 directory occupying the same premises. Now it is just a memory.

No. 236 Langsett Road was occupied by Horsfall's. Being near to Cuthbert Bank with its many pigeon cotes provided the shop with a plentiful supply of customers. They also sold equestrian and gardening supplies. I used to go there for nuts and corn as we had most of the collared doves in Ecclesfield to feed.

This corner greengrocery was to be found where Cuthbert Bank Road met Bamforth Street. I went looking for the site recently and found only weeds and trees where once it stood. The prices on the window are pre-decimal and the date is 1968.

This is Cuthbert Bank Road between Bamforth Street and Burton Street. Don't go looking for it. I did and I found that this once public highway has now been taken over by a private company and completely fenced off. I wonder what happened to all the people who once lived here.

Possibly they were re-housed in some of the flats that have also been demolished.

Here's a paradox - The Victorian landlords built for profit and created communities. The planners built for a caring society and created ghettos.

Burton Street. It runs from Langsett Road down to Penistone Road. Half way down on the left is Burton Street School that featured in the film "The Full Monty" It is all that is left of the buildings in this photograph. The rest were demolished in the early 1970s.

This is Hillsborough's
lost Street. Its correct name is
Montagu Road but it has now been renamed
Capel St. In the second house down my mother learned that
her first husband had been killed in the 1914-18 war.
The whole family used to gather here every Christmas Day until
it seemed the tiny room would burst. Grandma Witheford - my
maternal grandmother raised a large family in this house.
She was born in 1850!

No. 296 Langsett Road was the Cuthbert Arms pub. Being both a pub and a beer-off shop was rather unusual. Most pubs had an off-licence and some a separate counter for beer to take out but to have a separate shop attached was rare. I believe the only other such was the Catherine Arms in Catherine Street, Pitsmoor.

This is the interior of the Cuthbert Arms shop. It was common for a wife to go with a jug to fetch a working father's supper beer. Notice the three draught beer pumps. At one time children would also be sent and commonly tasted the contents which led to the beer act under which beer had to be supplied to children in sealed bottles.

This is Langsett Road at Greaves Street. People are waiting to see the first electric tram go past. It also shows two lost pubs, The Hampden View Hotel and the Royal Hotel. The date is 1903. In the 1905 directory these pubs are simply listed as beerhouses.

The Lyceum Hotel was situated at 153 Langsett Road.
To the right is King James Street. The photograph was taken in 1970.

No. 115 Langsett Road. The Bee Hive Inn was near Creswick St. before you get to Primrose Hill. The landlord at the time of this photo was David Michael Beckett. The poster advertises the 1968 film "Witchfinder General".

Primrose Hill is now a stop for Supertram. St. Bartholomew's Church and schoolroom loom large. This massive complex has now gone and been replaced with a medical centre and modern flats. The church entrance was on Burgoyne Road. Primrose Hill filling station has now closed. It played a small part in the film "The Full Monty",

Langsett Road at Wood Street with, on the left, the Wellington pub and across Wood Street one of the many pawnbrokers who helped the poor to survive. The date is around 1902.

Wood Street is the extent of my Hillsborough area. It runs from Langsett Road to Hillfoot Bridge. The street is now unrecognisable from how it was in the 1960s when this photograph was taken. All these houses have gone.

This is how Penistone Road used to be - a glorious mixture of little shops, houses, pubs and industry.
Wood Street is to the left. The date is around 1920.

Waiting for a tram on Penistone Road.
It is just appearing into the picture.
The date is the 1920s.

Penistone Road. These houses were demolished in the 1930s to provide a site for the New Barrack Tavern. The shop survived until more recent times.

Cuthbert Bank overlooks Penistone Road. It provided a site for a number of pigeon cotes. At the time of the photograph in the early 1980s travellers' caravans had occupied the grass verges taking advantage of the grazing opportunities. The dual carriageway runs where the horse is tethered.

A view from Cuthbert Bank showing the density of housing around Penistone Road. The roads are from left to right: Rawson Street, Woodgrove Lane, Fawley Road and Hicks Road. The photograph was taken around 1968.

This rare photograph shows the married quarters attached to Hillsborough Barracks. After the army departed in 1930 they were let for domestic use but were demolished in the 1970s. At the time of the photo the Barracks belonged to Burdalls.

On the left is Burton Street at its junction with Penistone Road with the little corner shop at No. 579. This was demolished for road widening in the 1980s. The photo was taken on 23rd July 1974.

On the right the 1983 Sheffield Marathon is streaming along Penistone Road towards Hillfoot Bridge. The date is 19th June. It was a hot day and there were some collapses.

Penistone Road from Parkside Road. All these buildings have been demolished. Opposite Hillsborough Park was a thriving residential area prior to the 1980s. The road on the right was Dutton Road.

Hillsborough National School stood where Woolworth's now stands. The path running off to the right led to the Blue Ball pub and was a short cut to Bradfield Road. To prevent it becoming a right-of-way it had to be closed for one day every year. It is now blocked off completely.

NATIONAL SCHOOL · HILLSBRO · 101.  FUR

This shot of Middlewood Road was taken before the shopping centre was built and shows those shops that were to disappear to make room for it. The date is Christmas 1977.

Middlewood Road at Crookes Place, now Procter Place. For many years this corner was owned by Wigfalls but now they have gone and that once well-known name is no more.

A group of shops on Middlewood Road as they were around 1932. The directory for that year gives the following details: No. 46 William Burton - fruiterer; No. 48 John Moule - oatcakes and pikelets; No. 50 Herbert Tesh - draper; No. 52 Ernest Mason - ironmonger; No. 56 George Sutherland - baker.

Roselle Street off Middlewood Road is shown at Christmas 1977.
The barrow lady with her holly wreaths is doing a brisk trade.
Procter Place is just visible in the background.

Middlewood Road at Hillsborough Park was experiencing a rainy day in 1927. There was no shelter for the tram driver on this particular type of tram.

Hillsborough Lake and bandstand. This bandstand was demolished after the war like others in the city. Very few now remain and those that do are in a sorry state. Band concerts in the park were a delight but I doubt that they would be big draws today.

This photograph of Bradfield Road dates from 1968. The church was Hillsborough Methodist Church. I remember that it was used to house bombed-out victims following the Blitz of 1940. I was sent there in my Church Lads' Brigade uniform to act as a messenger boy. The pub was, of course, The Shakespeare - an old Victorian pub now called "The Shakey". The shop was Burtons that had the slogan "Let Burtons Dress You".

A rather different view of Bradfield Road. We are standing on Fred Wilson's motor car sales forecourt. The church has gone and Burton's windows are boarded up - whether through vandalism or renovation I do not know. The Shakespeare stands where it has stood for many years.

This postcard is date-stamped 1907. On the right is Bush's grocer's shop. The site was later to become Burton's the tailors. On the left is the Hillsborough Inn.

This was Hillsborough tram terminus when this photograph was taken. The date would be around 1905. Prince.M. Sunderland's shop occupied Nos. 4 to 8 Langsett Road. He is described as a watchmaker in the 1905 directory.

"SCOTT" SERIES, No. 1039.

. Hillsborough corner around 1908 looking from Middlewood Road towards Barrack Hill.

Holme Lane has not changed all that much but the back-to-back houses in this picture were demolished many years ago. The old tram sheds are now a medical centre. The date of the photograph is 1968.

Situated at No. 270 Langsett Road the Mason's Arms is a Victorian pub. It still survives though all around it has gone and it now stands in splendid isolation. New houses on the opposite side of the road have provided a new clientele. The picture dates from 1979.

A view from Cuthbert Bank taken with a rather longer lens than normal to bring out details of how the area around Hillfoot Bridge used to be. On the right of the picture is Philadelphia School where I first developed my skills in woodwork - I don't think. We were sent there from Malin Bridge School clutching our tram tokens. It has now been demolished. Note the Town Hall in the distance.

Hillsborough Park again. We used to call this the old man's hut. It was demolished twenty or more years ago. During the war and the blackout it was popular with courting couples - the park railings had gone to help the war effort!

The Hillsborough Show of 1979. This must be the last time a band was heard in Hillsborough Park. Thereafter the Council, in its wisdom, decided the British armed services were not welcome in Sheffield. "Soldiers in the Park"? Not in our city.

Hillsborough Park has always had a thriving bowls club. This match was taking place in 1977.

This sweet shop stood at the bottom of Wadsley Lane and was excellently placed to catch cinemagoers heading for Hillsborough Park Cinema. The Phoenix poster was offering "Gold is Not All" and "The Whispered Word" but my efforts to date these films have been unsuccessful.

Here is Hillsborough Park Cinema in its days as a Bingo Hall. Sadly I failed to get a photograph when it was a cinema. I remember the excitement when Fred Astaire and Ginger Rogers appeared in "Top Hat" - "Oh you must go and see it!" My mother hastened down to the Thursday afternoon matinee. Matinees were held on Thursdays because it was early closing day for shop assistants.

The south-east corner of Bradfield Road was for many years Fred Wilson car lot. It was redeveloped in the 1980s and now contains shops, a bank etc. This is how it looked in the early 1980s.

Bradfield Road at Hawksley Avenue as it was around 1930. The large building centre left was Eagle House. The building on the extreme left was Hawksley Avenue sub-station that supplied direct current for Sheffield's tramways. My father was the attendant there and on the occasions I went in the place the noise was deafening. One wall was covered with voltmeters. At the Hawksley Avenue end there were huge turbines spinning away. He shared the job with his brother - 6am to 2pm was the morning shift and 2pm to 10pm was the afternoon shift. Each week they would reverse shifts.

This was Mr. Hawksley's mill on Bradfield Road after it had borne the force of waters from the Dale Dike reservoir following the flood of March 1864. It stood where the flats now stand. It is interesting to note that it had an undershot wheel. These were uncommon although there is another example at Malin Bridge. I believe that Hawksley Avenue was named after him.

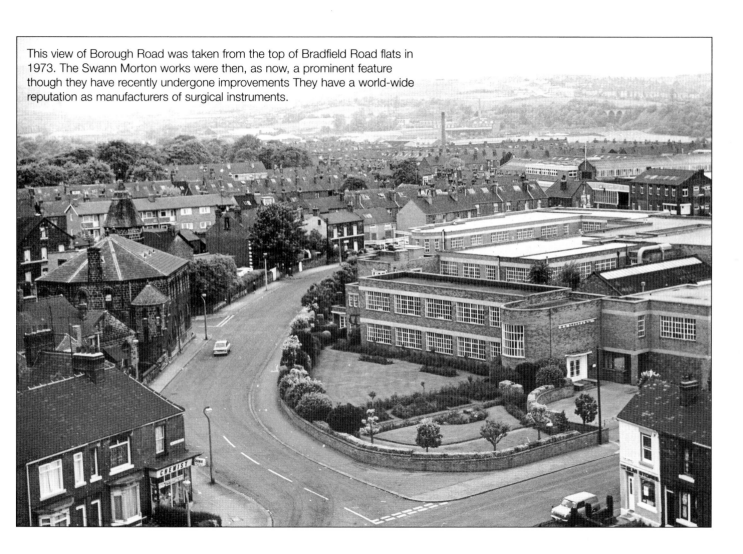

This view of Borough Road was taken from the top of Bradfield Road flats in 1973. The Swann Morton works were then, as now, a prominent feature though they have recently undergone improvements They have a world-wide reputation as manufacturers of surgical instruments.

At the corner of Borough Road and Owlerton Green these teenagers and their bikes face terraced houses that have long since been cleared. The photograph was taken in 1978 so these youngsters will now be approaching their forties.

A view of Owlerton from Bradfield Road flats taken in 1970. Owlerton Forge occupies the site that is now B&Q DIY store and across Penistone Road is Eaton & Booth's tilting and forging mill.

Another view from Bradfield Road flats showing Owlerton Green. Beyond is Owlerton Stadium built on what was once Owlerton village green. Most of the buildings in the foreground have now been demolished. The date is 1973.

The Freemason's Arms pub still stands at the bottom of Walkley Lane. The Sheffield Flood could not shift it. Here the pub landlord, Alfred Michael Firth poses with his staff.

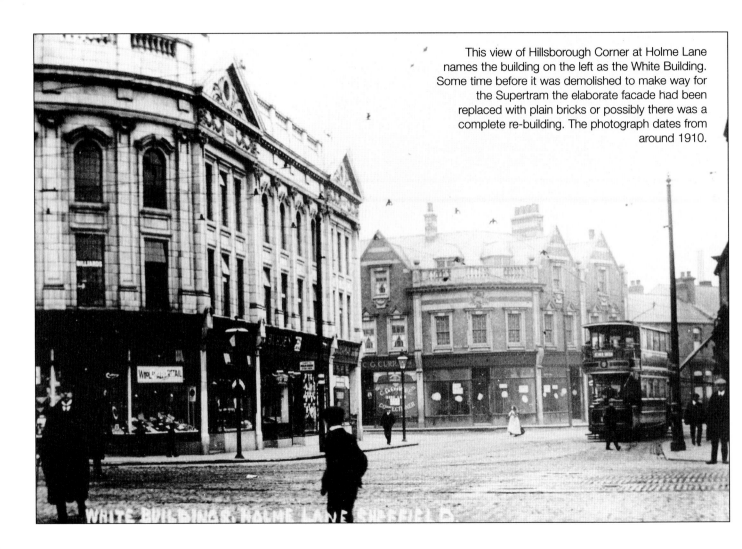

This view of Hillsborough Corner at Holme Lane names the building on the left as the White Building. Some time before it was demolished to make way for the Supertram the elaborate facade had been replaced with plain bricks or possibly there was a complete re-building. The photograph dates from around 1910.

WHITE BUILDINGS, HOLME LANE SHEFFIELD

Hillsborough Corner before Supertram. The shops on the left had to go so that the tram could turn into Langsett Road. Compare this photograph with previous page and you will see that those white buildings bear no resemblance to these. It must be that at some time this block was rebuilt  The date of this photo is 24th July 1983.

Holme Lane around 1914. The tram is passing back-to-back houses that were a common sight in Sheffield before the War. Virtually all of them - these included - have now been demolished.

Holme Lane at Malin Bridge in 1968. On the left is St. Polycarp's tin hall. Both sides of the road have now been demolished. Everything on the left was cleared to make way for the one-way system and a slip road now runs where Polly's tin hut once stood. Who now remembers the sixpenny hops on Saturday nights with the three-piece band?

Burgon and Ball Limited, manufacturers of sheep and garden shears (according to the 1915 directory). This was their works at Malin Bridge as they were in 1968. The River Loxley runs alongside. All this has now been cleared.

This is a pleasant photograph of Malin Bridge tram terminus as it was around 1910. Milk was delivered from the milk can straight into the housewife's jug - more often a gill (half-a-pint) than a pint. A drink of milk was a luxury before school milk started.

MALIN BRIDGE. SHEFFIELD. 556

Malin Bridge around 1910. The Rivelin Valley Road bridge had not long been built. In the distance is the countryside that was to become the Wisewood Estate. Johnny Wood's works can be seen as can Wisewood Lane with the little chapel where we had magic lantern shows and pease pudding.

Leppings Lane gets its name from the old "lepping" or stepping stones where it crosses the River Don. This photograph is dated 1881. The Wednesday ground would be built to the right of this scene.

This was the Hillsborough platoon of the Home Guard posing for their photograph at the Wednesday Ground. Far from being the Dad's Army as depicted on television most of these look nearer Pike's age than Jones's. Can you spot your grandad?

This is how the Wednesday ground looked in the 1970s. Notice the undeveloped state at the bottom of the picture.

The photo was taken at Hillsborough at 3.50 p.m. on September 2nd 1911, the opening day of the 1911-1912 football season. The Wednesday were beaten 1-0 by Preston North End. Owls fans can take some consolation from the fact that Wednesday finished fifth in the old First Division that season and Preston were relegated. The team was: Davison (in goal) Brittleton, Campbell, Kirkman, McLean, McSkimming, Paterson, Robertson, Spoors, Weir and Wilson.

A goalmouth incident when Wednesday played Mansfield Town on 30th October 1976. Chris Turner (now Wednesday's manager) is in goal for this Third Division clash that Mansfield won 2-0. The rest of the team that day was: Bradshaw, Dowd, Collins, Feeley, Henson, Hope, Johnson, Walden, Wylde and Jefferson (who was on temporary loan from Wolves).

What would a cup semi-final be without the partisan favours. It can be a dangerous occupation and this entrepreneur appears to have adopted a bi-partisan approach. I can spot two different kinds of scarf which, in 1977, meant Man United and Leeds.

The F.A. cup semi-final for 1977 was played at Hillsborough. The police had their hands full on this occasion as can be seen from this photo taken on Penistone Road.

This alarming photograph was also taken at the F.A. cup semi-final of 1977. It shows a disaster waiting to happen. Had those railings collapsed there would have been injuries if not deaths. At the final whistle Manchester United had beaten Leeds United by 2-1.

During the 1977 F.A. Cup semi-final at Hillsborough Manchester United fans who had been unable to get into the ground were causing trouble at the Leppings Lane entrance. Mounted police are attempting to protect the gates.

Hillsborough's own Niagara Falls was situated where Law Brothers filling station now stands. The Niagara Sports Ground, owned by Sheffield Police, is the site of the dam that fed this weir.

Where Herries Road North meets Penistone Road there is a busy traffic roundabout. This is how it looked in less frantic days. The house stood at the end of Leppings Lane. The date is difficult - possibly the 1920s.

Across the road there was the Sheffield Corporation bus depot. This photograph was taken in 1974 before buses were privatised and when Sheffield had a cheap fares policy. If I remember rightly the fare from Ecclesfield to Sheffield was then no more than ten pence. It is now £1.35.